SOMETHING TO SAY

A Stage Play in One Act

by Richard Everett

‖SAMUEL FRENCH‖

samuelfrench.co.uk

Copyright © 2018 by Richard Everett
All Rights Reserved

SOMETHING TO SAY is fully protected under the copyright laws of the British Commonwealth, including Canada, the United States of America, and all other countries of the Copyright Union. All rights, including professional and amateur stage productions, recitation, lecturing, public reading, motion picture, radio broadcasting, television and the rights of translation into foreign languages are strictly reserved.

ISBN 978-0-573-11592-9

www.samuelfrench.co.uk

www.samuelfrench.com

FOR AMATEUR PRODUCTION ENQUIRIES

UNITED KINGDOM AND WORLD
EXCLUDING NORTH AMERICA
plays@samuelfrench.co.uk
020 7255 4302/01

Each title is subject to availability from Samuel French,
depending upon country of performance.

CAUTION: Professional and amateur producers are hereby warned that *SOMETHING TO SAY* is subject to a licensing fee. Publication of this play does not imply availability for performance. Both amateurs and professionals considering a production are strongly advised to apply to the appropriate agent before starting rehearsals, advertising, or booking a theatre. A licensing fee must be paid whether the title is presented for charity or gain and whether or not admission is charged.

The professional rights in this play are controlled by Samuel French Ltd, 24-32 Stephenson Way, London NW1 2HD.

No one shall make any changes in this title for the purpose of production. No part of this book may be reproduced, stored in a retrieval system, or transmitted in any form, by any means, now known or yet to be invented, including mechanical, electronic, photocopying, recording, videotaping, or otherwise, without the prior written permission of the publisher. No one shall upload this title, or part of this title, to any social media websites.

The right of Richard Everett to be identified as author of this work has been asserted in accordance with Section 77 of the Copyright, Designs and Patents Act 1988.

THINKING ABOUT PERFORMING A SHOW?

There are thousands of plays and musicals available to perform from Samuel French right now, and applying for a licence is easier and more affordable than you might think

From classic plays to brand new musicals, from monologues to epic dramas, there are shows for everyone.

Plays and musicals are protected by copyright law, so if you want to perform them, the first thing you'll need is a licence. This simple process helps support the playwright by ensuring they get paid for their work and means that you'll have the documents you need to stage the show in public.

Not all our shows are available to perform all the time, so it's important to check and apply for a licence before you start rehearsals or commit to doing the show.

LEARN MORE & FIND THOUSANDS OF SHOWS

Browse our full range of plays and musicals, and find out more about how to license a show
www.samuelfrench.co.uk/perform

Talk to the friendly experts in our Licensing team for advice on choosing a show and help with licensing
plays@samuelfrench.co.uk   020 7387 9373

Acting Editions

BORN TO PERFORM

Playscripts designed from the ground up to work the way you do in rehearsal, performance and study

---

Larger, clearer text for easier reading

Wider margins for notes

Performance features such as character and props lists, sound and lighting cues, and more

---

+ CHOOSE A SIZE AND STYLE TO SUIT YOU

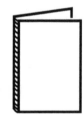

STANDARD EDITION

Our regular paperback book at our regular size

SPIRAL-BOUND EDITION

The same size as the Standard Edition, but with a sturdy, easy-to-fold, easy-to-hold spiral-bound spine

LARGE EDITION

A4 size and spiral bound, with larger text and a blank page for notes opposite every page of text – perfect for technical and directing use

LEARN MORE | samuelfrench.co.uk/actingeditions

Other plays by RICHARD EVERETT
published and licensed by Samuel French

Close To The Wind

Entertaining Angels

Present from the Past

Hand Over Fist

Happy Event

FIND PERFECT PLAYS TO PERFORM AT
www.samuelfrench.co.uk/perform

ABOUT THE AUTHOR

Richard Everett is an actor, playwright and screenwriter. He is the author of six published stage plays including the much-acclaimed *Entertaining Angels*, which has had over a hundred productions worldwide. He has two hundred animation scripts to his credit as well as two feature films, three plays for BBC Radio 4, and a published collection of award-winning sketches and meditations entitled *Sound Bites*. He is a Visiting Fellow of St John's College, Durham University.

Richard also runs drama workshops for Additional Needs Adults and seminars on 'The Writer's Journey'.

More information can be obtained from his website: www.richardeverett.co.uk

Photograph credit: Kate Kennington Steer

AUTHOR'S NOTE

Infidelity in drama is a well-trodden path so in that respect I make no claim for originality of theme in this play. What I did want to explore was the less likely response of a partner on the receiving end of a confession of unfaithfulness from their other partner. Such confessions are not uncommon and people do it for different reasons. In the case of Maddie, I ask the question: is it because she genuinely wants a new life? Or is it because it's preferable to being found out and she somehow thinks that by confessing all to her husband she will be licensed to continue? Or, more intriguingly, is it her coded way of asking to be rescued from something she has got herself into and doesn't know how to get out of? I will leave the cast to ponder and come to their own conclusions. I think I know what I think.

What is even more interesting to me is David's reaction. When I first wrote this play for Radio 4, my literary agent said the only thing he didn't believe was the husband's instant decision to go with his wife and confront her lover. My response to my agent was the same as the note I gave the actor playing David: think of being involved in a car crash and the moment immediately after when the injured driver, oblivious to his cuts and bruises and attendant pain, has a brief window of being incredibly practical and detached. In short, just for a few moments the shock enables him to function on automatic. That is David's state of mind when Maddie ambushes him with her confession. So, keeping the lid on David's emotions is the key to playing him, and it is only in the last few minutes of the play that he starts to bleed and fall apart. If all of the preceding scenes are played with an unexpected, almost menacing calm and stillness it will make David's final surrender to his true feelings very powerful. It will also make him a more intriguing character to observe as we, with Maddie, try to interpret his odd and clinical reaction to her news. Put simply, he becomes dangerously interesting and unpredictable.

I confess that Stephan and Jane are 'feeds' to this story but their roles are indispensable. Jane needs to be caught between being the responsible listening friend giving grounded advice, and the re-awakened teenager enjoying a vicarious fantasy through the recklessness of her best friend. Stephan needs to be somewhat bemused by the sudden intrusion into his pad on this particular evening, and how someone else's marital crisis seems to be spilling onto his living room carpet. In other words, although David addresses much of what he says to Stephan, he is really talking over Stephan's head to Maddie. One might imagine Stephan closing the door after this disturbed couple have left and asking himself 'what the hell was that?' – and then returning either to the book he was reading, or carrying on watching the TV programme he put on pause when the doorbell rang earlier.

There is some dark comedy to be found in this short piece, but the key to that is, as always, to play it for real. To date, whenever I have done an after-show q&a session with audiences, the response has been exceptionally good – as well as divided in where their sympathies lie. That to me is the greatest compliment and the most satisfying response – with tears and laughter coming a close second!

Thanks for choosing this play. I hope it makes for an interesting journey for all concerned.

Richard Everett, 2018.

MUSIC USE NOTE

Licensees are solely responsible for obtaining formal written permission from copyright owners to use copyrighted music in the performance of this play and are strongly cautioned to do so. If no such permission is obtained by the licensee, then the licensee must use only original music that the licensee owns and controls. Licensees are solely responsible and liable for all music clearances and shall indemnify the copyright owners of the play(s) and their licensing agent, Samuel French, against any costs, expenses, losses and liabilities arising from the use of music by licensees. Please contact the appropriate music licensing authority in your territory for the rights to any incidental music.

IMPORTANT BILLING AND CREDIT REQUIREMENTS

If you have obtained performance rights to this title, please refer to your licensing agreement for important billing and credit requirements.

"SOMETHING TO SAY"

Something To Say was originally written for BBC Radio 4 Afternoon Drama.

It was first presented as a stage play by 3tc (Teignmouth Touring Theatre Company) on 25th May 2018 at The Ice Factory, Teignmouth, with the following cast:

MADDIE	Rebekah Hayden
DAVID	David Warren
JANE	Lydia Dockray
STEPHAN	Mason Castree

Directed by Jackie Wesley-Harkcom
Production by Philip Wesley-Harkcom

CHARACTERS

MADDIE – aged mid thirties
JANE – a friend, aged mid thirties
DAVID – Maddie's husband, aged late thirties
STEPHAN – aged mid twenties

SETTING

David and Maddie's sitting room
Stephan's house and the street outside

TIME

The present

MADDIE *and* **DAVID**'s *sitting room.*

The sets throughout can be as elaborate or as abstract and spare as production resources allow using the same furniture and exits and the fourth wall suggesting a real working fireplace. There is an upstage exit to an unseen kitchen and another to an unseen hallway and front door.

The lights come up on **MADDIE** *and* **JANE** *deep in conversation over coffee, either sitting on the floor staring at the fire or at a dining table staring at their coffee mugs. A pause as* **JANE** *considers what she has just been told. Then...*

JANE What can I say?

MADDIE Nothing.

JANE I wish I could think of something to say.

MADDIE There's nothing. It just helps having someone to listen.

JANE Oh Maddie.

MADDIE I know. I feel such a fool.

JANE How old did you say he is?

MADDIE Twenty five...

    JANE *reacts.*

MADDIE ... 'ish.

    They both giggle.

JANE Well, at least he's legal. He is legal, I hope?

MADDIE Of course he's legal!

JANE You said "'ish", that's all.

MADDIE Come on, I'm not that stupid.

JANE Well, so long he's old enough to know what he's getting into. Is he very good looking?

MADDIE Stop it.

JANE What! I'm just asking.

MADDIE Yes. He is.

JANE Well...don't rush, that's all.

MADDIE Rush where?

JANE Into anything. I know you – just don't...rush.

MADDIE I didn't ask for it to happen, you know.

JANE No, I know. God, whoever would have thought it though?

MADDIE What?

JANE You! You're the last person!

MADDIE I'm not that unattractive.

JANE No. It's just...

MADDIE It's not a crime, Jane.

JANE I'm not saying that... Oh, I don't know Maddie – what can I say?

MADDIE Nothing. Every Mills and Boon is stuffed full of it. It's happened, I just have to deal with it.

JANE And you're sure?

MADDIE About what?

JANE Look, I don't want to pry but have you actually...you know...

MADDIE What?

JANE Done it, slept with him. You implied earlier that it hadn't got that far.

MADDIE Did I?

JANE Yes.

MADDIE Oh.

JANE Oh my God.

MADDIE I don't recall having time to actually sleep.

JANE Oh my God.

MADDIE All afternoon, on his living room sofa.

JANE Oh my God.

MADDIE I know.

JANE How wonderful.

They grin at each other like teenagers.

I'm sorry, that's not at all helpful. For God's sake, Maddie – are you absolutely sure?

MADDIE Oh yes, he has a small birthmark on his right shoulder.

JANE Come on, I'm being serious.

MADDIE I know, I know. Every time I close my eyes and say, "Come on Maddie get a grip", all I see is the pattern of his living room wall paper moving rhythmically back and forth.

JANE You've got it bad, girl – you know that?

Pause. They both sip coffee and stare at the fire again.

I have to say... I had no idea you and David were having problems.

MADDIE We're not.

JANE Well...not happy, then.

MADDIE We are.

JANE Happy.

MADDIE Yes.

JANE Sorry, I'm lost.

MADDIE *looks at her quizzically.*

Why are you screwing the kid in the pine shop, Maddie?!

MADDIE His name is Stephan, Jane – and he is not a kid.

JANE But why?

MADDIE And we're not screwing each other we're in love.

JANE You know what I'm saying. What is this actually about?

MADDIE Does it have to be about anything? It is what it is.

JANE Which is this: you walk into a furniture shop, a pretty young boy flashes a smile at you, buys you a couple of drinks...

MADDIE Coffee actually. Flat white.

JANE Flat white, how appropriate. And three weeks and a pine table later, you're flat out on his sitting room sofa getting cushion burn and watching his moving wallpaper. Pretty reckless and pretty wonderful, but it happens. Is it anything more than that?

MADDIE Yes – it's happened to me!

JANE Well, 'happened *to* you' is debatable but the bigger question is – what are you going to do about it?

MADDIE I can't pretend I don't feel what I feel.

JANE I know that and I'm not unsympathetic, truly I'm not, but if you're going to continue with it – are you going to continue with it?

MADDIE Well, yes – duh!

JANE Then here come the questions, honey – tough ones too. Like...do you want to move in with him?

MADDIE He hasn't actually asked but I think he'd like me to. He won't rush me though, he won't ask until he thinks I'm ready, he's very sensitive like that.

JANE Is he. And are you ready?

MADDIE Probably not, no.

JANE But you're thinking about it?

MADDIE Yes.

> JANE *looks at her, at a loss.*

Please tell me you understand.

JANE Of course I understand. What woman wouldn't but... Oh I don't know, I really don't. Seriously though, what about David?

MADDIE What about David, indeed.

JANE Will you tell him?

MADDIE He is my husband. Deceit only makes it worse, don't you think?

JANE How do you think he'll react?

MADDIE God knows.

JANE You think he'll want you to leave?

MADDIE I doubt it – there's the children to consider.

JANE Yes, quite. You think he'll want to leave, then?

MADDIE Possibly. Maybe my marriage is over, Jane – maybe this is as far as David and I can go.

JANE I find that hard to believe.

MADDIE Really?

JANE Yes, actually – I do.

> *Brief pause.* MADDIE *looks defeated.*

Come here, I want to give you a hug.

> *They hug. As they do...*

Daft cow. I wish I could think of something to say... I tell you this though – there isn't a single married woman who hasn't, at some stage...

MADDIE *breaks off the hug...*

MADDIE Wait.

JANE What?

MADDIE Say that again.

JANE Well, I hadn't finished...

MADDIE A single married woman.

JANE What?

MADDIE Three weeks ago I was a married married woman and now I feel like a single married woman.

JANE Oh. Right. And that helps, does it?

MADDIE Don't you see?

JANE Not really, because what I was trying to say...

MADDIE That's how I feel, Jane!

JANE For goodness sake woman, will you listen for a moment?! ...There isn't a single married woman who hasn't, at some stage, either seriously considered or even just toyed with doing what you're doing.

MADDIE *tries to follow the relevance of this.*

MADDIE So, what – you're saying I'm weak now? Is that it?

JANE No! I'm saying you're not alone.

MADDIE This wasn't just a high street pass – we talked, we laughed, we connected...and then...well...

JANE He got his leg over.

MADDIE He entered my life.

JANE And who opened the door?

MADDIE Yes, I accept that.

JANE So, close it?

MADDIE It is closed – he's already inside.

JANE Then open it again and show him out?

MADDIE I'm not sure I can. Like a photograph – you can't un-take it.

Pause.

JANE What do you *want* to do, Maddie? If someone were to wave a magic wand, what would you want to happen?

MADDIE I'd like...everything to stay as it is because I don't want to hurt David or my children...and I'd like no one to mind or take the blindest bit of notice.

JANE And leave you alone in your happy world of pine shops and patterned wallpaper?

MADDIE Yes please.

JANE Well, I'm fresh out of magic wands, I'm afraid... Oh, good grief, the time – I have to collect the kids!

MADDIE Shit! I have to collect Sam!

MADDIE *exits with the two mugs to the kitchen while* JANE *starts putting on her coat.*

JANE Doesn't Erica do it?

MADDIE *(offstage)* It's her morning off. She goes to English classes.

JANE *(calling)* Or so she says – she's probably down at the pine shop, as we speak!

JANE *laughs at her joke then regrets it as* MADDIE *reappears.*

Sorry. That wasn't funny or clever.

MADDIE You've been a friend and a brick, honey – thank you.

They hug.

I suppose you'll tell John, will you?

JANE Not if you don't want me to. When will you tell David?

MADDIE Tonight probably.

> **MADDIE** *exits to get her coat.*

JANE Well, if there's anything I can do.

MADDIE *(offstage)* You can make up your spare bed just in case!

> **MADDIE** *reappears pulling on her coat.*

JANE I do understand hun, you know that?

MADDIE I'm glad someone does because I don't.

> **MADDIE** *reaches into her coat pocket, pulls out a bunch of keys.*

JANE In fact...

MADDIE What?

JANE Nothing.

MADDIE Oh for goodness sake – I can't bear it when you do this!

JANE I really rather envy you.

MADDIE For God's sake woman, get a grip.

> **MADDIE** *pushes* **JANE** *towards the door and they exit.*

> *Blackout. Music. Lights come up on...*

> *The same. Evening.*

> **DAVID** *enters opening a bottle of wine. He calls to* **MADDIE** *in the kitchen.*

DAVID I'm just opening another, okay? ...Maddie?

MADDIE *(offstage)* What?!

DAVID You look stressed, I thought we'd crack open another.

MADDIE *(offstage)* Not for me! I won't be long – I'm just loading the dishwasher!

DAVID Leave it. Erica can do it in the morning.

MADDIE *(offstage)* I don't mind!

> DAVID *pours himself a glass of wine.*

> *Beat.*

> *He stands and warms himself in front of the fire.*

> MADDIE *enters.* DAVID *raises his glass and gestures to the wine.*

DAVID Sure?

MADDIE Um...yes, all right.

> MADDIE *also warms herself.* DAVID *pours a second glass.*

DAVID How is Sam doing at the new nursery?

MADDIE Okay – seems to be. It's Chloe I'm worried about.

DAVID I liked her painting, by the way. For a six-year-old, very good I thought.

MADDIE I hope you told her, she was very proud of it.

DAVID Of course. So why are you worried?

> DAVID *hands her the glass.*

MADDIE I don't know, she's a funny little girl. She told me today some boys in the playground had told her to take down her knickers and show her bum.

DAVID You're joking. Maddie, that's a reportable incident.

MADDIE It's all right. Further investigation revealed it was just a dream.

DAVID I'm not sure that isn't worse.

MADDIE And then she blushed and ran out of the room.

DAVID I don't blame her, I'd blush and run out of the room if I owned up to a dream like that. Cheers.

DAVID clinks her glass.

MADDIE Yes. Cheers.

DAVID You know what Sam said to me in the bath yesterday? He eyed me for a long time and then said: "You've got a willy, Mummy's got boobies and in the summer I'm going to have a bicycle with peggles!"

They laugh. MADDIE sips her wine and sits. He remains standing.

MADDIE Are you going to sit?

DAVID Sorry?

MADDIE I was just wondering if you were going to sit.

DAVID Where?

MADDIE Here. With me.

DAVID Probably. What do you want me to do – stand in the hall? *(Suddenly playacting)* Come my dear, let us both sit together by the fire!

He takes her hand and kisses it elegantly. She pulls it back irritated.

MADDIE For goodness sake.

He sits beside her and smiles at her affectionately.

I want to talk to you – seriously.

DAVID I can run to a serious conversation. What about?

MADDIE What about?

DAVID Yes.

MADDIE Right. Well.

DAVID Sorry, sorry to stop your flow but is it all right if I sit here or would you rather I sat over there?

He loons about shifting seats.

MADDIE David, please stop, I'm trying to be serious.

DAVID I'm just concerned about the seating arrangements!

His buffoonery is not working.

I'm sorry, it's the wine... I'm all yours.

MADDIE I don't really know how to begin with this but...what is it now?!

DAVID *bursts out laughing.*

DAVID I'm sorry, I'm sorry!

MADDIE Always taking the piss, you are.

DAVID It's just, your face.

MADDIE What's wrong with my face?

DAVID Nothing's wrong with your face. I love your face, but when you're trying to be serious – it goes all serious.

MADDIE I'm not trying, I am being serious. Anyway, so do you.

DAVID What?

MADDIE Have a serious face.

DAVID Do I?

MADDIE Yes.

DAVID How do I look?

MADDIE I don't know.

DAVID Show me.

MADDIE Can we stop this now? It's important what I want to discuss.

DAVID If you show me, I'll make the coffee.

MADDIE Oh for...! Look, if I show you, will you at least agree to listen to what I have to say?

DAVID You have my word.

MADDIE Well...you sort of go —

DAVID laughs as she demonstrates.

DAVID Really?

MADDIE Yes. And sometimes you even go...

She demonstrates again.

DAVID Really?

MADDIE Stupid, if you ask me. Oh, this is hopeless. You're not in the right frame of mind.

DAVID For what?

MADDIE Go and make the coffee.

DAVID Not until you've got whatever it is off your chest. I tell you what – I'll help. On a scale of one to ten, how serious is it?

She doesn't answer.

Five? ...Seven?

MADDIE Nine and a half.

DAVID Right. Okay. Subject – does it involve us, the children, or someone else?

Pause. MADDIE sighs. She looks at him, then...

MADDIE All three.

DAVID I see – we're not at war, are we? Only, I missed the seven o'clock news.

MADDIE David!

DAVID Sorry, sorry. So, we've got a nine point five's worth of bad news about you, me, the children and someone else. Yes?

Brief pause.

MADDIE Yes.

DAVID Okay, go for it.

MADDIE You'll be shocked.

DAVID Shock me.

MADDIE I mean, really shocked.

DAVID Really shock me.

MADDIE Have you noticed a change in me at all?

DAVID What sort of change? My God. You haven't fallen for the au pair, have you?

MADDIE *just stares at him...*

She is a head-turner.

MADDIE I'm having an affair, David.

Pause. DAVID *stares at her stunned and expressionless.*

You want me to say it again?

DAVID No. I heard you the first time.

His expression turns to an icy stare.

Now?

MADDIE What d'you mean 'now'?

DAVID You said 'having'. You mean it's going on now?

MADDIE Well, not this instant. I'm here with you, aren't I?

DAVID *laughs a brief hollow laugh.*

What? You think it's funny?

DAVID No. I don't.

MADDIE Then why did you laugh?

DAVID It wasn't jocular, I assure you. I'll put the kettle on.

MADDIE What?

DAVID I believe that's what one does in situations like this.

He sets off towards the kitchen...

MADDIE David, I've just told you...

He stops at the doorway...

DAVID That you're having an affair. Yes, I heard you.

He exits. **MADDIE** *buries her face in her hands.*

MADDIE *(to herself)* What am I doing, what am I doing?

DAVID *reappears...*

DAVID White or black?

MADDIE Will you please say something?

DAVID I just did.

MADDIE Black.

DAVID exits again, then calls from the kitchen...

DAVID *(offstage)* You like sugar if you're having it black, don't you?

MADDIE *doesn't respond.* **DAVID** *sticks his head round the door.*

MADDIE Please say something – even if it's piss off.

DAVID Piss off.

MADDIE Not very convincing.

DAVID Not really meant. Or would you prefer sweetners? I'll do sweetners.

DAVID vanishes.

MADDIE Don't you want to ask 'who'?

No response.

David?

DAVID *re-enters with two mugs.*

DAVID I've gone for instant – I can't be arsed to fanny around with a filter.

He hands her a mug. She takes it. He remains standing and watches her.

Of course I do. I also want to ask – when, where, how long it's been going on...and why? But I also don't want to know.

MADDIE No. Of course.

DAVID However, as we've reached the point of no return, we'd better continue. By the way, how did you envisage this little fireside chat – with me here and you there, or the other way round?

MADDIE You're not making this very easy.

DAVID How thoughtless. Let's just sit where we are then, shall we?

He sits.

So. Been out shopping, have we?

MADDIE That's an awful expression.

DAVID You choose a better one.

MADDIE I've fallen in love with someone else.

DAVID Have you. Well, let's leave the who and the why to one side for a moment, shall we?

MADDIE Why are you being so clinical?

DAVID Well, forgive me for saying so, but you've just dropped a hand grenade in my lap and I'm trying to see if the pin's still in it.

MADDIE I appreciate that but...

DAVID I'm trying not to panic, sweetheart. What would you prefer – that I burst into tears and throw something?

MADDIE It might help.

DAVID Who?

MADDIE Either of us.

DAVID Rubbish. Anyway it would wake the children.

MADDIE Never mind the children, just be honest, be yourself.

DAVID Is that what you're hoping I'll say to you – never mind the children just be yourself?

Pause.

MADDIE Just...ask what you like.

DAVID How long?

MADDIE Nearly a month.

DAVID Is that all?

MADDIE You wish it were longer?

DAVID Is this the first time?

MADDIE Yes.

DAVID Never before?

MADDIE Never.

DAVID Where did you meet him – it is a 'he', I assume?

MADDIE Yes. The pine shop. He works there.

DAVID What, the one up the road?

MADDIE Yes.

DAVID Convenient.

MADDIE What's that supposed to mean?

DAVID Saves on petrol.

MADDIE Do you think I planned it? You think I woke up one morning and said: "I know! Let's go to the pine shop and get laid"?

DAVID Didn't you?

MADDIE No! I did not!

DAVID You didn't get laid?

MADDIE Yes, of course I got...!

> MADDIE *stops herself but it's too late.*

I'm sorry, I didn't mean it to come out that way. This is horrible.

DAVID Yes. Isn't it just.

MADDIE You're being very cruel.

DAVID To whom?

MADDIE To yourself, actually.

DAVID You think soft words and fireside tears would make this easier?

MADDIE You're making it sordid.

DAVID It is sordid.

> *Pause. They sip their coffee and stare at the fire.*

MADDIE I had no intention of being unfaithful to you.

I did not plan it and I'm trying to avoid being deceitful.

DAVID I know you are. You're not cut out for this at all. How old is this man?

MADDIE Twenty five...ish.

DAVID Ish?

MADDIE Yes, but I have to say...

DAVID If you say "But he's very mature for his age" I *will* throw something. And you've known him a month?

MADDIE Three weeks.

DAVID And you've been with him – how often?

MADDIE You mean...?

DAVID Yes, I mean exactly that. How many times?

MADDIE Once.

DAVID And now you're in love.

> DAVID *stares at her, still expressionless.*

MADDIE I'm sorry, David.

DAVID *(cracking slightly)* What the hell's going on, Maddie?

MADDIE Would it help if I told you how I feel.

DAVID No thanks. It's not me that's in trouble.

MADDIE How do you mean? Coming to terms with something like this must be tough.

DAVID For who?

MADDIE For you. Why am I having to spell everything out?

DAVID Let's get something clear. It's not me that has to come to terms with anything, Maddie – it's you. And it will be painful.

MADDIE Obviously, I feel guilty inflicting an injury like this...

DAVID No. Sweetheart, you're not listening. This isn't about me. We're not going to get anywhere with this if you don't start facing yourself.

MADDIE I am.

DAVID You're not in love with this boy.

MADDIE How do you know, how can you say that?

DAVID Because I know.

MADDIE Well, you're wrong.

DAVID And he's not in love with you, either.

MADDIE Look, I know it's hard for you to accept...

DAVID Accept what? So far all I've heard is a load of magazine drivel about you and the boy in the pine shop. We've got to get at the truth and we have to do it together. I can't stand here with my feet on the ground if you're floating about in the stratosphere.

MADDIE But everything I say, you say is untrue.

DAVID Okay, maybe I'm being a bit ham-fisted, but can we try and get some perspective here? You say you've met this man who you find very attractive...and... *(His voice cracks again)* ...You've slept with him.

MADDIE Oh God.

DAVID No, I'm alright. Now. In the three weeks you've been seeing him your feelings have blossomed into something deeper – even love. Yes?

Beat.

MADDIE Yes.

DAVID Good. Right. And now you've told me – which, incidentally, I regard as an act of considerable courage, a lot of wives would have done different.

MADDIE And husbands.

DAVID And husbands, indeed. So you've confessed all, nothing's hidden. Where do we go from here?

MADDIE Where do you suggest?

DAVID Stop making this everyone else's problem, Maddie! You have to decide.

MADDIE You'll let me decide?

DAVID No one else can do it for you.

MADDIE What if you don't like it?

DAVID I'll resist. Play every card I've got.

MADDIE Why do I have to decide anything now?

DAVID Because you chose to bring it up now.

Pause. MADDIE *looks away from him, takes a breath. Then...*

MADDIE I want to move in with him.

DAVID Good. Excellent. Now we're getting somewhere. I say you're mad.

MADDIE I can't help it.

DAVID You'll be back in a week.

MADDIE Maybe.

DAVID You'll distress the children, kill off your marriage and damage yourself irrevocably

MADDIE Not necessarily.

DAVID Grow up, woman.

MADDIE I can't help myself, David. I think of him all day long, I'm in love with the little bastard.

DAVID Oh God, Maddie – you ran through a few corn fields together! You can't carve up your marriage and screw up your children because of a roll in the hay! Talk sense, for God's sake!

MADDIE You're extraordinary, you stand there like some sort of forensic scientist analysing a specimen. I have feelings and emotions, David. I don't expect sympathy but you could at least try and understand.

DAVID I do. That's the problem.

MADDIE You haven't the faintest clue what I'm going through. If you did...

DAVID If I did, what?

MADDIE You'd be asking the obvious – you'd be asking if there was a reason for this.

DAVID Is there?

Beat.

MADDIE I don't know.

DAVID I don't think so – nothing complicated anyway. You looked at another man, he looked at you and you fancied each other. Millions of people do that every day, the only difference is you went a step further.

MADDIE But I'm *feeling* something!

DAVID Of course you're feeling something, you're a human being. But it isn't love.

MADDIE You don't know that. And even if it isn't love, doesn't the fact that I think it is, tell you something?

DAVID Yes. It tells me that I've failed. It tells me that it's far too long since I told you I loved you – which, incidentally, I do – but people make that mistake every day. If you say it's more than that, I say you're giving it a significance it doesn't deserve. Life is simple, Maddie – it's people that make it complicated.

MADDIE There is nothing simple about the way I feel.

DAVID Look, as sexual beings, men and women are not naturally monogamous. You get married but you still find other people attractive – deeply so at times. It's perfectly natural. It's also perfectly natural to fall flat on your face in the street but it's not the normal way to get about. The normal way is upright and on two feet. People like us get married to normalise a situation that would otherwise be chaos.

MADDIE And who says romance is dead? "Marry me, darling! I need to normalise a situation that would otherwise be chaos!"

Pause. She looks at him. He holds her gaze.

DAVID It isn't love, Maddie. And I don't believe there is anything wrong with our marriage.

MADDIE I feel...so confused. I honestly don't know what to do.

DAVID Well, you've fallen flat on your face on the pavement – you've torn your tights, your knees are bleeding and you're a bit shaken. What do you want to do?

MADDIE Cry.

DAVID Then do it. And then brush yourself down and move on.

MADDIE So cold. So callous. How do you do it?

DAVID The only way out of this mess is if one of us hangs onto the truth. If I let my feelings get the upper hand, we'll both disappear up our emotional arses – and that's when the rot really sets in. We'll be two more victims on the road to destructive misery – and all because one of us fell over in the street. Is that what you want? If it is, you're not only careless but stupid.

MADDIE Oh, fuck off.

DAVID The stakes are too high. We have two nodding heads asleep upstairs.

MADDIE I said: fuck off, will you?!

DAVID Go and tell them that you're walking out because Mummy gave the kid up the road a bit of the old 'dippy-dippy'.

MADDIE You unfeeling bastard!

DAVID You've been had – you've been had by the boy in the pine shop... What's his name again?

MADDIE Stephan.

DAVID Yes, of course it is.

MADDIE What do you mean?

DAVID His name, Stephan – it had to be.

MADDIE Why?

DAVID Wears a denim shirt, does he? Open to about here. (*pointing to his chest*)

MADDIE No, actually. He wears a chunky fisherman's jersey that smells of varnish – look, what has this to do with anything?

DAVID In my day it was a denim shirt. Jeans and cowboy boots?

MADDIE Do you know him or something?

DAVID *laughs*.

DAVID Oh Maddie, Maddie!

MADDIE You do, don't you?

DAVID Like the back of my hand.

MADDIE Are you playing games with me?

DAVID I'm the only one dealing you a straight hand here. If, by 'knowing', you mean in the biblical sense, then no, I've left that privilege to you.

MADDIE Do you know Stephan, have you ever met him?

DAVID Yes, I know him but no I've never met him... Oh, Stephan, Stephan, Stephanovitch!

MADDIE *looks at him and is at a loss.*

MADDIE What are you trying to do to me?

DAVID I'm trying to find you, that's all.

DAVID *galvanises into action and reaches into the hall returning with two coats.*

Here put this on.

He throws her coat at her, she catches it.

MADDIE What for?

DAVID It's cold.

MADDIE Where are we going?

DAVID To pay him a visit.

Beat. **MADDIE** *stands motionless holding the coat.*

MADDIE Don't be so bloody stupid.

DAVID Erica's in her room, isn't she? I'll tell her to keep an ear open.

DAVID *exits leaving* **MADDIE** *still frozen to the spot...we hear* **DAVID** *calling out.*

(*offstage*) Erica? We're just popping out! We shouldn't be long!

DAVID *reappears, head round the door.*

Well, come on! Don't just stand there!

He reaches for the light switch.

Blackout. Music.

Lights fade up as **MADDIE** *stands in the same position but now wearing her coat.*

The street outside **STEPHAN**'s *front door.*

MADDIE This is absurd.

DAVID *enters speedily scanning the street, apparently looking at door numbers.*

DAVID Number...twelve you said?

MADDIE I'm not telling you.

DAVID *eventually peers through an imaginary window upstage.*

DAVID Aha! Yes! Got to be. There's an Annigoni over the fireplace with a stripped pine surround.

DAVID *leans on the door bell which we hear.*

MADDIE I'm not doing it. I'm not coming in.

DAVID Yes you are.

MADDIE Ridiculous. I feel about ten years old.

DAVID And stop lurking under that tree. You look like a stalker.

MADDIE I hate you, I absolutely hate you.

> STEPHAN *appears, a quietly spoken young man with the hint of a Yorkshire accent.*

STEPHAN Yes?

> *He looks at* DAVID *not knowing who he is. Then he sees* MADDIE.

Maddie?

DAVID Hello. I'm the husband. May we come in?

STEPHAN Oh my God.

DAVID Excellent.

> DAVID *doesn't wait for an answer, he just pushes through the doorway and exits.*

> MADDIE *looks at* STEPHAN *and shrugs.*

MADDIE Sorry. Nothing I could do.

> MADDIE *pushes past him and also exits into the house.* STEPHAN *now alone on his doorstep, looks up and down the street to see if there is anyone else, then also enters the house.*

> *Lighting changes to:*

> STEPHAN's *sitting room.*

> DAVID *enters the same set but from another entrance as we are now inside* STEPHAN's *house.*

DAVID Sitting room through here is it? ...Oh very nice! Yes, very cosy indeed.

STEPHAN *and* MADDIE *follow, hovering in the doorway.*

STEPHAN Is he a hitter?

MADDIE How the hell should I know? It's never happened before.

DAVID Charming! Absolutely charming! Now, before you say anything, my apologies for turning up unannounced, this was entirely my idea... Why have you take your glasses off?

MADDIE He thinks you're going to hit him.

DAVID Ha! No, no. Good heavens, I'm not that sort, Stephan. Relax – please. I'm nervous enough as it is, if we both stand here quaking we'll go through the floor together. Jolly nice knock-through, by the way – solid job. Did you do it?

STEPHAN The people before.

DAVID Did they. Splendid. You can make such a hash of knocking through. Anyway, it's reassuring to meet you face to face. When one's wife announces she's taken a lover one immediately pictures a muscle-bound brute with a huge adam's apple – like in one of those aftershave adverts? ... No? Before your time, maybe. Anyway, you're not like that – more the artsy type, I imagine.

MADDIE David?

DAVID Yes darling?

MADDIE Shut the fuck up.

STEPHAN Look, Mr...?

DAVID David, please.

STEPHAN *offers his hand to shake.*

STEPHAN Stephan.

DAVID *looks at the hand being offered.*

DAVID I don't think so, if you don't mind?

STEPHAN *withdraws his hand awkwardly.*

Now, this won't take long, I just want to get a few things
out in the open so we all know where we stand. No need
for hysterics. This isn't 'High Noon', it's just after supper
and I have to be up early for a meeting. I understand you've
been screwing my wife.

MADDIE Oh God.

DAVID Sorry darling. Did you say something?

MADDIE David, what are you doing?

DAVID Getting things out in the open? I thought I said.

MADDIE I'm not a lump of meat, you know.

DAVID No, I don't think you are. Do you, Stephan?

STEPHAN Sorry?

DAVID Think she's a lump of meat? Maddie's concerned we
think she's a lump of meat.

STEPHAN Of course I don't think that.

DAVID Good. We're agreed on something already. All going
frightfully well. By the way, I couldn't help noticing this
table – beautiful workmanship.

STEPHAN I made it myself.

DAVID *caresses it admiringly.*

DAVID Did you really? That's amazing. Have you seen it darling?
Quite superb. Well, I'm sure you have on your previous
visits. Now then...

MADDIE David, please could you stop this?

STEPHAN May I just say something?

DAVID Yes, go ahead.

STEPHAN I don't quite know what has or hasn't been said but
seeing as you're here and seeing as you're not looking for
a fist fight, perhaps I could...well...explain a few things?

DAVID Do, if you want but it isn't necessary.

STEPHAN Well, I thought a little perspective...

DAVID Perspective. Yes. We talked about that, but your perspective, my perspective, Maddie's perspective – what the hell. It all comes down to the same thing in the end, don't you agree?

STEPHAN It depends what you mean.

DAVID Do you love my wife?

> *Pause.* MADDIE *looks at* STEPHAN *who looks blank.*

> Come on, it's a simple enough question. Do you love her?

> STEPHAN *looks at* MADDIE.

STEPHAN Yes.

DAVID How much?

STEPHAN What kind of a question is that?

DAVID Practical.

STEPHAN You can't measure love in that way.

DAVID Yes you can. Do you want her to come and live with you?

STEPHAN I'm not sure.

MADDIE I feel sick.

DAVID Try and hold on if you can, sweetheart, and if not I'm sure you know where the bathroom is.

STEPHAN If that's what she wants.

DAVID You love her enough to have her come and live with you. I see, and if I told you she's been screwing around with other men – would you still want that?

MADDIE For God's sake, David.

STEPHAN What other men?

MADDIE Don't believe him.

DAVID Other men. Does it matter?

MADDIE I've no idea what he's playing at.

DAVID If you knew she'd been screwing even one other man at the same time as you, would you still want her to come and live with you? Yes or no, Stephan?

STEPHAN Probably not, no.

DAVID Ah. Well. You see. There's the difference – I would. And she has been screwing around – with you. And I still want her to live with me – and so do my son and daughter. All three of us – that's how much we love her. You see?

STEPHAN Maybe Maddie has had enough of all that. Maybe she wants out.

DAVID Fair point. Let's ask her. On second thoughts there's no need – she does. At least, she thinks she does.

STEPHAN But you know better?

DAVID Too damn right. She's my wife, I've known her for fourteen years and until you came along the thought of leaving never entered her head.

MADDIE You don't know that.

DAVID Did it?

Beat.

MADDIE No.

DAVID Of course it didn't. Let's not play games, the stakes are far too high and way above your pay grade, Stephan. What's more, I know you better than you think.

STEPHAN What's that supposed to mean?

DAVID Where did you do it? Upstairs – or down here in front of the fire?

MADDIE Stop it David.

DAVID Come on, Stephanovitch – 'fess up!

STEPHAN What kind of pervy question is that?

DAVID You wouldn't use the floor, not with all these rugs and bare boards – you'd get splinters or carpet burn. I know, I'll wander round the house...

DAVID *wanders exaggeratedly about.*

...and you can tell me if I'm getting hot or cold.

MADDIE David, this is disgusting.

STEPHAN You really want to know, don't you?

DAVID I've asked you three times.

STEPHAN Right here. On the sofa.

DAVID This one?

STEPHAN That's it.

DAVID This one here?

STEPHAN That one there.

DAVID What was wrong with your bed?

STEPHAN It happened on the sofa.

DAVID Bit risky moving from here to the bedroom, was it? Afraid she might change her mind on the stairs?

STEPHAN We did it on the sofa.

DAVID You did it on the sofa.

STEPHAN She enjoyed herself.

DAVID You screwed my wife.

STEPHAN We spent time together, we laughed and listened to music.

DAVID Of course you did! You're a sensitive young man. You're not the sort who grabs the first married woman that walks into his shop and pins her up against a Victorian sideboard.

You're a man of taste, if you're going out for a meal you want the full four courses.

STEPHAN I'm not listening to any more of this.

DAVID I'm not passing judgement, Stephan. You're not into underage girls or getting a woman drunk, and the last thing you want is to hurt anyone. Right?

STEPHAN Right.

DAVID And if an attractive woman crosses your path, someone who appreciates nice things like stripped pine and a quiet drink...well, where's the harm in that?

STEPHAN Right.

DAVID And if you discover she's married but still willing to go the distance, who are you to go digging around in her domestic life?

STEPHAN None of my business.

DAVID None of your business, absolutely. You're not a home breaker are you, Stephan?

STEPHAN Certainly not.

DAVID I expect you like kids – wouldn't mind a few of your own some day?

STEPHAN When the time's right.

DAVID When the time is right. And I'm sure you'll make an excellent father – one day. In the meantime, all you want is a discreet amount of pleasure given and received.

STEPHAN Like you said – I'm not a home breaker.

DAVID No. Neither was I.

STEPHAN *stares at him, trying to understand.* MADDIE *likewise.*

We're two of a kind you and I. Sixteen years ago I did exactly the same.

STEPHAN As what?

DAVID Oh come on, Stephanovitch. What are you – arrogant
or just naive? You seriously think you're the first man to
up-end a married woman?

MADDIE David?

DAVID Before I met you, darling – don't worry. Katy Mather
her name was. Thirty four, as innocent as they come, and
she fell into my arms like ripe fruit. But it didn't last and
the usual happened – husband found out, tears and threats
and we never saw each other again. She was divorced a few
years later, but... I don't think that had anything to do with
me. The marriage must have been rocky for her to be up
for it in the first place. I heard she remarried a couple of
times but never made a go of it. As I say, I'm sure it had
nothing whatever to do with me.

MADDIE You've never told me any of this.

DAVID Why would you want to know?

MADDIE You've spoken about other women before we were
married.

DAVID Yes. Well. Katy was a little bit special – because she was
the first, I suppose.

MADDIE There were others?

DAVID A couple more – but none of them came near the lovely
Katy. The others...well...they were a bit too good at it for my
liking. Had a taste for it, knew what they were doing, and
using me to get back at their husbands. Katy? She was the
real thing – so vulnerable...which made her so intoxicating.
So, you see Stephan – we're two of a kind. November the
fifth it's fireworks the rest of the year it's other people's
marriages. And now? Well, the tables are turned, aren't they?

STEPHAN Meaning?

DAVID I'm on the receiving end. Perhaps you will be one day.
All you want is some harmless masculine fun and I'm just

the heartless shit who's lashing out in all directions to save his marriage and protect his family. You two? You've got the heavy mob rooting for you – Coldplay and the Cointreau advert. What chance have I got? And with a past like mine, I can't even plead the innocent victim.

Pause.

STEPHAN So. What now?

DAVID What happens next?

STEPHAN Yes.

DAVID It's up to Maddie. It always was. Obviously I was hoping she might be moved by all that I've said – but I doubt it. I would have liked to have exposed you as a selfish, randy layabout – but you're not, so I'm out of aces. Not much more I can do apart from asking you to pack it in here and now. I appreciate that's not easy and I know there's the complication of us living up the road, but geography has little to do with this. It's a mindset. If Maddie can't see her way out, she'll fall prey to a dozen others. That's why it's pointless punching anyone – for every one of you I flatten there will be another ten waiting round the corner – like the good old Space Invaders, you keep on coming.

Pause. No one speaks or moves. **MADDIE** *is expressionless.*

Look...um... I'll go and wait outside. Take a few minutes on your own. And then I'd like it if Maddie came home with me.

STEPHAN Just like that.

DAVID There's no need to prolong this, is there?

STEPHAN That simple.

DAVID You've no need of each other.

MADDIE I disagree.

DAVID *and* **STEPHAN** *both look at* **MADDIE** *as she breaks her silence.*

DAVID Plenty more fish in the sea for Stephan, Maddie. And Stephan's a luxury you can't afford. The truth – if it wasn't you wouldn't be in so much pain.

MADDIE My pain, like my choices, is mine to do with as I wish, David. Whatever you think, and however well-meant, I do not need protecting – from Stephan, from preying men round the corner, or even from you...thank you very much.

DAVID Understood. But like all of us, Maddie, sometimes we need protection from ourselves. I'll wait outside.

MADDIE No. Don't. Go home.

DAVID I'd prefer it...

MADDIE I know what you'd prefer, David. I said, go home.

A moment as DAVID *tries to interpret this.*

I will come when I'm ready.

DAVID *hesitates.* MADDIE *watches him until he turns and exits.* STEPHAN *turns to look at her.* MADDIE's *gaze moves from the now empty doorway to* STEPHAN.

Blackout. Brief music.

MADDIE *and* DAVID's *sitting room.*

Lights come up slowly on DAVID *alone and crouched by the fire in the half-light. After a few moments* MADDIE *appears in the doorway with her coat on.*

You're still up?

DAVID *doesn't look round at her.*

DAVID I took the long way home.

MADDIE You must be exhausted.

DAVID You need to be more than tired to sleep.

MADDIE All quiet upstairs?

DAVID Sam was awake when I came in, his little antennae were out – said he felt sick.

MADDIE Was he?

DAVID No. I gave him a drink and stroked his head, he went out like a light.

MADDIE *takes her coat off and throws it on the floor. She crouches next to him in front of the fire. They both gaze at the flames. Then...*

You all right?

MADDIE Yes.

DAVID Really?

MADDIE Yes. I had a little cry, felt thoroughly sorry for myself...

She trails off. Pause.

DAVID Crying is allowed, you know.

MADDIE I know. But I left my tears on the pavement – together with my torn tights.

DAVID You don't have to pretend. I know it's only the beginning.

MADDIE Beginning?

DAVID You'll find yourself deliberately passing his shop on your way to the Post Office, and deliberately passing it again because you forgot to actually post the letter. There will be a hundred pointless excursions to the newsagent to buy magazines you don't want. You'll play all kinds of tricks on yourself.

MADDIE You think I'll make it?

DAVID To the newsagent and back? Yes. I do. Provided you don't rush – and trip.

Beat.

Tell me, if you want.

MADDIE You are an extraordinary man.

DAVID I don't think so.

MADDIE You think of everything.

DAVID It's the thinking I dread.

MADDIE What do you mean?

DAVID All those months ahead. Those moments.

She turns and looks at him. He still looks into the fire.

Moments to come. Thinking of everything – of you...and him...on that fucking sofa.

DAVID *hangs his head and weeps.* MADDIE *puts her arms round him and holds him like a child.*

MADDIE What can I say?

DAVID Nothing.

MADDIE I wish I could think of something to say.

She cradles him. Music. Lights fade slowly to black.

The End

FURNITURE AND PROPS LIST

Scene One
Sofa
Small dining table
Two dining chairs
Two coffee mugs
Coat and bunch of keys (Maddie off stage)
Coat and shoulder bag (Jane. Pre-set)

Scene Two
Wine bottle
Corkscrew
Two wine glasses
Two mugs of coffee (off stage)
Jacket (David)
Coat (Maddie)

Scene Three (Outside and inside Stephan's house)
Specs (Stephan)

Scene Four
Coat and bunch of keys (Maddie)

LIGHTING

Cue 1 – Scene One: Opening. As music fades lights up to late morning, bright sunshine.

Cue 2 – Scene One: Maddie: "For God's sake woman, get a grip!" As Maddie and Jane leave, fade to black. Hold for approx. ten seconds while music plays.

Lights up to Scene Two: Gentle evening with hint of warm glow from real fire.

Cue 3 – Scene Two: David: "Well, come on! Don't just stand there!" As he leaves and Maddie remains, slow fade to black. Hold for approx. ten seconds while music plays.

Lights up to Scene Three: Cold night, street.

Cue 4 – Scene Three: As Stephan follows David and Maddie into his house, slow crossfade to...

Warm interior of Stephan's house, and David: *(Entering)* "Sitting room through here is it?"

Cue 5 – Scene Three: David leaves. Maddie and Stephan are alone. Slow fade to black. Hold for approx. ten seconds while music plays.

Lights up to Scene Four: Maddie and David's home as before but subdued half-light with maybe just the glow of the fire, as Maddie enters.

Cue 6 – Maddie: "I wish I could think of something to say." Very slow fade to black as extended music plays. Hold while music resolves.

Cue 7 – Lights full up for cast call.

SOUND AND EFFECTS

Cue 1: Opening music. Fade out as lights come up.

Cue 2: Maddie: "For God's sake woman, get a grip!" – fade up music. Play through blackout then slow fade out as lights come up again.

Cue 3: David: "Well, come on! Don't just stand there!" As he leaves and Maddie remains, fade up music. Play through blackout then slow fade out as lights come up again.

Cue 4: David: "Aha! Yes! Got to be. There's an Annigoni over the fireplace with as stripped pine surround."

Sound Effects: Long aggressive ring on doorbell.

Cue 5: Maddie: "I'll come when I'm ready." David leaving, Maddie and Stephan alone. Fade up music and play through blackout then slow fade out as lights come up again.

Cue 6: Maddie: "I wish I could think of something to say." Gentle fade up of music. Play into blackout until music resolves.

THIS
IS
NOT
THE
END

**Visit samuelfrench.co.uk
and discover the best
theatre bookshop
on the internet.**

A vast range of plays
Acting and theatre books
Gifts

samuelfrench.co.uk

samuelfrenchltd

samuel french uk